Play

Protect Your Life!

Self Protection for Everyone

by

Master Dominick Ruggieri

Published by China Hand Kung Fu Academy, LLC www.chinahand.com

Note: The information in this book is true and complete to the best of our knowledge. This book is intended only as an informative guide for those wishing to know more about self protection issues. Information in this book is general and is offered with no guarantees on the part of the author or China Hand Kung Fu Academy, LLC. The author and publisher disclaim all liability in connection with the use of this book.

For more information visit our website at www.how2playthegame.com

Order this book online at www.trafford.com
or email orders@trafford.com

Most Trafford titles are also available at major online book retailers.

Printed in Victoria, BC, Canada.

ISBN: 978-1-4269-2181-0

Our mission is to efficiently provide the world's finest, most comprehensive book publishing service, enabling every author to experience success. To find out how to publish your book, your way, and have it available worldwide, visit us online at www.trafford.com

Trafford rev. 12/10/09

 www.trafford.com

North America & international
toll-free: 1 888 232 4444 (USA & Canada)
phone: 250 383 6864 ♦ fax: 812 355 4082

Play The Game ~ Protect Your Life!!!

Self Protection for Everyone

Dominick Ruggieri

Table of Contents

Preface

After 25 years of training in the Chinese Martial Arts and personally experiencing the benefits that are received from practicing them, I want to share these great arts with everyone to the level of passion they want to learn them too. I want to provide everyone with the ability to protect themselves from predators and those who commit random acts of violence. By giving back to the community; I can "pay it forward."

This book will teach you to "Play The Game" so you can "Protect Your Life." By relating simple movements to typical life experiences, we will show you how to use what you already know in order to remember the skills needed to "Protect Your Life." In turn, you will gain confidence. By providing you with the tools and confidence needed when confronted, you can Act.

In teaching martial arts to such a wide variety of people and wanting to provide protection tools to the average person, some tribulations were encountered. First, a complicated underlying principle needed to be made so simple, everyone could understand it. Second, coordination problems needed to be eliminated. Third, people needed to gain confidence quickly. Fourth, it needed to be used easily by everyone from age 5 – 75. And fifth, they needed to be doing it in minutes without learning countless techniques that are technical and complicated.

It seemed as soon as I broke one barrier, I hit another. The process continued over and over. Considering most of what I have learned took hours of practice year after year, it felt like I was never going to break through the barrier.

Then, one day, from out of the blue, I was inspired while playing with my son, Dominick. With an idea in mind I tried doing it with him. Within 10 minutes of playing with Dominick I came up with The Game. Since that day, he has been my test audience and my motivation to continue on.

I broke all of the barriers because you are reading this book.

Acknowledgements

Like all acknowledgements, it is impossible to recognize all of the people that it truly takes to bring a project like this together. Nor do I think that I can thank everyone the way I would like too. In any event, to everyone, thank you for your patience, support and understanding and for providing me the energy to have a vision be realized.

To my family for putting up with me, the journeys I take, and where they lead me. You have always supported me and gave nothing but encouragement.

Without my students this would have been an even more difficult task. To my instructors who assisted in teaching classes, to the students for being patient through the process, and to everyone for putting forth the positive support encouraging me to continue on.

Friends are students; friends are parents of students, friends are those who know me from other parts and times in my life, you are many. It is all of you that I thank from the bottom of my heart. I owe all of this to a special friend. Without you this book would have never materialized. It was your motivation that started the momentum, thank you.

Acknowledgement has to go to the several instructors from the Peter Kwok Style of Kung Fu.

First and foremost, though never studying directly under your tutelage, I would like to take this moment to recognize and thank you for your undying commitment to kung fu. Without your willingness to share these arts with the world and thereby producing quality instructors, I would have never have reached this goal. Grandmaster Peter Kwok, we owe you thanks, gratitude, and appreciation.

Patrick Hanvey and Mark Gates, my first instructors, started it all. They nurtured my training and started me on this special path. If they had not been there, none of this would have been possible. They toiled over hours of lessons to be sure I understood the material and held me to a high standard, yet allowed me to still progress at my own rate. I also owe them thanks for understanding and supporting me when I wanted to expand my knowledge, go to other instructors, and improve myself. It is their perseverance that has led me to where I am today.

Randy Elia, who's open mindedness, took me in as a student of the Peter Kwok system and treated me like a long term student even though I had learned from different teachers. Once again, I found nurturing and caring in his teaching style that encouraged me to work hard, want to be better, and lead me to the next level of my training.

To Gary Torres, yet another instructor from the Peter Kwok system who was willing to share. He continued to refine, provide understanding, encourage, and open his arms to me in an effort to keep a high level of understanding and quality that is so prevalent in the Peter Kwok system.

All of my instructors had created a relationship that fostered being friends, mentors, and more importantly, family. Each of you provided a level of understanding in order for me to grasp a concept while accepting and respecting my methods and teachings. My school and teachings are a part of each of you. Thank you.

About The Author

Dominick Ruggieri was born 1960 in Lakehurst, New Jersey and grew up at the Jersey Shore. He is the oldest of 5 children. Dominick was named after his grandfather Dominick Nersita whom he loved to spend time with.

Dominick has two beautiful children which are his inspiration; Nichole age 19 and Dominick age 13.

Dominick's martial arts training began with an adult education class. This led him down the path to a higher level of training in the traditional Chinese arts of Shao Lin Kung Fu, Tai Chi, Pa Kua, Hsing Yi, Chi Kung, Weapons, Chin Na and Massage Therapy.

After 6 years of training, under the tutelage of his instructors, Patric Hanvey and Mark Gates, founders of China Hand Kung Fu Academy, he started teaching adult education classes in Tai Chi and later became a partner in the Academy. Dominick continued training under Patric and Mark for over 20 years.

He has also studied under Master Randy Elia and Master Gary Torres. Dominick has taken numerous workshops and seminars with other well known masters in the Chinese arts such as Leo Fong, Y.C. Wong, Lou Die Xiu, Gao Zian, Yang Fu Kui, and Henry Look.

Dominick has judged at local, national and international tournaments for 10 years with students receiving gold, silver, and bronze medals. He was on the Board of Directors for the Guang Ping Yang Tai Chi Association and served as its president. Dominick has been nominated into three Masters Halls of Fame and received honors as the Best Kung Fu School in Ocean County, NJ.

While working full-time, training, and teaching part time, Dominick had the vision of opening his own Academy branch. Then in 1993, this vision was realized and China Hand Kung Fu Academy opened its' second Academy in Brick, New Jersey. In 1998, Dominick fulfilled another dream and began teaching martial arts as a full-time profession. Today he continues to provide group and private instruction at his Academy to students ranging from 5 years old to 85 years old.

Dominick's website provides general information and virtual training instruction. He has also produced a series of instructional DVD's that supports the Academy and website. To date, the website has over 1,100 video clips and 50 volumes of instructional DVD's and both are still growing. Instruction is being provided worldwide as result of these efforts.

Introduction

Let me pose this question. Why do you need or want to learn self protection? We are taught from pre-school and kindergarten age how to handle conflict resolution. We learn Kelso's Rules and how to deal with bully's by talking our way out of a situation; the list goes on. But, what are we teaching, or learning, for the occasion when these options fail?

Why are you sending your children to martial arts classes? Why are you taking a self defense class? Is it because you want to be able to protect yourself in the event conflict resolution doesn't work? Is it so that you can protect yourself if someone attacks you without notice or provocation? I would venture to say the answer is yes.

I agree with and support the notion that we should exhaust all avenues of non-physical conflict resolution first before we use a self protection method. However, sometimes you are not given the chance or the choice.

I want the average person to have the ability to protect themselves to whatever level they choose.

After you Play The Game, take a moment and see if the coordination is like anything you do anywhere in your daily routine or activities. By recognizing similar movements in different situations or activities you are always practicing Play The Game, thereby making it second nature.

This leads to an infinitesimal number of ways and methods for you to apply Play The Game without you having to preplan for each and every possible situation. You only need one way and that one way is Play The Game.

A family friend, Tim, was going to the bank in a very safe town where the violent crime rate is very low. He has his little 5 year old daughter in the back seat. He pulls into the bank and another car pulls up beside him and taps his car and scratches it. A woman was driving with her boyfriend in the passenger seat.

Tim gets out of the car to talk to the driver, who denies hitting him. The boyfriend gets out of the passenger side of the car, comes around and punches Tim in the face. Unprovoked, no warning, and out of no-where this random act of violence occurred.

Now, Tim is left no alternative but self protection. He has his little girl in the back seat of the car. The last thing he wanted to do was get into a fight, let alone fight with his daughter there, watching, observing and in possible jeopardy.

Did I mention the guy who hit Tim was a little guy, Tim lifts weights, is rather large, and someone that you would normally not want to fight. But, strange things do happen.

Below is one simple example that was brought to me by someone who has Played The Game.

Carla, one of my students came into class and we were just chatting. She said, "You know, The Game is just like turning the steering wheel on the car to turn. One hand over the other and one hand over the other again."

What is Play The Game ~ Protect Your Life?

Simply put Play The Game ~ Protect Your Life is a game that is FUN. This simple game, played between two people, of any age, teaches self protection without the need for costly lessons and in depth understanding of fighting concept and theory. Certainly, if you want to pursue these avenues, they are excellent.

Play The Game ~ Protect Your Life is about learning how to prepare you, your children, your parents, college co-eds, loved ones, or anyone you care about, how to protect themselves when facing danger and are in need of self protection. As we go through different stages of our lives, these needs change. When we are a child, it is dealing with the bully in the neighborhood, on the bus, or in school. Going to college and starting to socialize as young adults; what happens when a party gets out of hand, someone loses their temper, you meet the school yard bully – but now only older. Of course there are even more situations like mugging, robbery, car jacking, kidknapping, rape, or the random violence that is, unfortunately, just a part of everyday life.

In order to build your confidence and to prepare you for the situations that life presents to us, there is Play The Game ~ Protect Your Life. Play The Game is simple and can be easily incorporated into everyday life. Play The Game is fun. So consider this: if you could be shown a fun way to understand how to protect yourself while leaving out all of the concept, theory, complicated practice, and years of traditional training by using a game, would you do it?

Now, by drawing upon your life experiences, you already have the tools to use and if relating to those tools makes learning easy, fun, and simple wouldn't you want to learn how to Play The Game? If I said your kids will like to play it with you, would you do it? If I told you this is not a new concept to martial arts but just a new approach to cut to the chase, would you do it? What if I said even if you have self defense training, I could get you to understand your previous training even better, would you do it? If I take away all of the reasons why you shouldn't and couldn't do it, then all you have to do is have FUN.

How many parents learn CPR or Basic First Aid when they have children in order to prepare themselves for a time they may need to use these skills?

In 17 years of knowing CPR, I have never used it, but I am prepared. In 17 years of first aid classes, I have used some, but not even close to all, or even half of what I learned.

Preparation in life can save you (and your loved ones) from harm. People stereotype others everyday by their physical features. Many people are told everyday that they are too small and too shy to protect themselves. Overcoming these attributes and learning to protect yourself when a situation presents is what Play The Game ~ Protect Your Life intends to teach. Many people tell me "I couldn't hurt someone else." Well then let me ask you this, if the occasion arose, could you perform CPR or do emergency first aid to someone? Or, would you just let someone die? I don't know the answer for you because there are many difficult situations and considerations that are made in a split second. But, what if I said <u>"I know you could do it, I have faith that you could do it, and I trust in you"</u> when the time comes. What brings this confidence about? Those things that we do all the time, we become confident at doing. As a person, I believe you have it in you to want to protect your loved ones. So, just take a moment and "empty your cup," and let's put something fresh into it, you will be surprised.

Play The Game ~ Protect Your Life is about promoting confidence that will change the way you view protection forever. It will show that you have most of the tools already to protect you and your loved ones. You just need to be shown a way to use the tools in a different way. Play The Game ~ Protect Your Life is going to do just that.

Play The Game ~ Protect Your Life is already part of your daily routine. This allows you to be prepared to take action in a manner that is appropriate for the situation with no thought or effort on your part. Why, because when it happens it will be second nature.

There is only right in Play The Game ~ Protect Your Life. You need to dismiss the idea that making a mistake or doing the wrong thing will lead to trouble or something bad. You need to know that "You can do it!!!" Of course like all things in life, there is more than one way to do something. That is the attitude you need to take and will gain through Playing The Game. This game is meant to be fun. Make it fun and keep it simple.

To tell you a short story here, I had asked one of the Dad's who'd two sons take a class at my Academy, if he would do me a favor. The favor was to take this partially completed book, while at home one day, go to The Game Section, and try it with his 6 and 9 year old boys. They had not done it in class and had no idea what it was about. It was just to see if they could do any part of it without any prior training in The Game.

The following week they came to class. I asked how it went. He said "let us show you." One of the sons started doing it with Dad. They got it! I asked "how long did it take?" About 15 minutes was the answer. Then we started a short discussion. Without any of my prompting, the Dad started telling me about all of the things they were doing and explaining how he saw it working. He was correct, he understood the principle and his son wanted to play more.

To go even further, they were watching a documentary on the Discovery channel about fighting, martial arts and the like. They saw a scene in which a Chinese Kung Fu Master was practice fighting with a student. The Master was great and fast. But, the comment from the Dad was, I was just doing the same thing with my son an hour earlier. The Master was just doing The Game. The Dad and son had recognized the skills and what that Chinese Master was doing. Why? Because they had just finished doing the same skills by Playing The Game. Their confidence levels were very high, as they should have been. All this without me giving them one instruction other than a book that wasn't yet complete, not even pictures. Thanks guys.

Chapter 1
What's happening

Four measures of serious violent crime

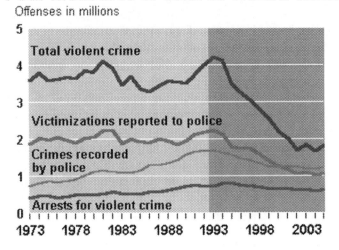

Offenses in millions

Total violent crime

Victimizations reported to police

Crimes recorded by police

Arrests for violent crime

In looking at the statistics and doing the research, the good news is that crimes in general have decreased over the last 10 years. On the other hand, it didn't go away; it is still there and will never go away. I bet right now, without even going beyond your family or close friends, you know someone who has had a crime committed against them at some level.

In an effort to have this chapter make sense, we will define some terms as they are used in the reports they were taken. All of these reports can be found online and we give you those references at the end of this book. This chapter speaks for itself and is for your information only.

Violent crimes are defined in the Uniform Crime Reporting Program as those offenses which involve force or threat of force. Such crime is composed generally of four offenses: murder and non-negligent manslaughter, forcible rape, robbery, and aggravated assault.

Aggravated assault is an unlawful attack by one person upon another for the purpose of inflicting severe or aggravated bodily injury. The Program further specifies that this type of assault is usually accompanied by the use of a weapon or by other means likely to produce death or great bodily harm.

Attempted aggravated assault that involves the display of—or threat to use—a gun, knife, or other weapon is included in this crime category because serious personal injury would likely result if the assault were completed. When aggravated assault and larceny-theft occur together, the offense falls under the category of robbery.

Overall

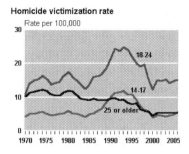

Homicide victimization rate
Rate per 100,000

In 2006, 1,417,745 violent crimes occurred nationwide, making 473.5 crimes per 100,000 people.

Aggravated assault accounted for 60.7% or 860,853 violent crimes. This is 287.5 offenses per 100,000 people. Robbery accounted for 31.6% of violent crimes. Forcible rape accounted for 6.5% of violent crimes. Murder accounted for 1.2% of violent crimes.

Males were more likely to be violently victimized by a stranger than a non-stranger. Females were more likely to be victimized by a friend, an acquaintance, or an intimate. In 2002, 30% of the victimizations involved an offender who had been drinking.

Intimate Crimes

Intimates were identified by the victims of workplace violence as the perpetrator in about 1% of all workplace violent crime. Two-thirds of victims who suffered violence by an intimate (a current or former spouse, boyfriend, or girlfriend) reported that alcohol had been a factor. Among spouse victims, 3 out of 4 incidents were reported to have involved an offender who had been drinking.

In 2005, about 40% of the victims of nonfatal violence in the workplace reported that they knew their offender. About 1 in 320 households were affected by intimate partner violence. Female victims are more likely to be victimized by intimates than male victims. About seven in ten female rape or sexual assault victims stated the offender was an intimate, other relative, a friend or an acquaintance.

Of offenders victimizing females, 18% were described as intimates and 34% as strangers. By contrast, of offenders victimizing males, 3% were described as intimates and 54% as strangers.

77% (18.0 million) were property crimes

1% (227,000) were personal thefts

Children

In 2005, U.S. residents <u>age 12 or older</u> experienced approximately 23 million crimes, according to findings from the National Crime Victimization Survey. For every 1,000 persons age 12 or older, there occurred

- 1 rape or sexual assault

- 1 assault with injury

- 3 robberies

Murders were the least frequent violent victimization -- about 6 murder victims per 100,000 persons in 2005 out of 22% (5.2 million) of violent crimes.

The website Talking With Kids in conjunction with Nickelodeon, the Kaiser Family Foundation and Children Now is to get kids and parents talking. They report:

"BULLYING, DISCRIMINATION AND SEXUAL PRESSURES "BIG PROBLEMS" FOR TODAY'S TEENS AND YOUNGER KIDS; PARENTS OFTEN WAIT FOR THEIR KIDS TO RAISE TOUGH ISSUES."

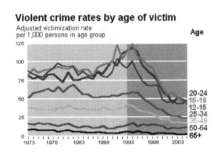

Violent crime rates by age of victim
Adjusted victimization rate per 1,000 persons in age group

Large numbers of 8-11 year olds say teasing and bullying (74%), discrimination and disrespect (43%), and threats of violence (38%) occur at their school. One third of 10-11 year olds (33%) say that pressure to have sex is a "big problem" for kids their age. Yet, many parents still put off talking about tough issues with their children, according to a new national survey of parents and kids.

School Crimes

Between 1992 and 2005, crime in the Nation's schools for students ages 12-18 fell, a pattern consistent with the decline in the national crime rate.

Again this is good news. But look what is still happening: In every year from 1992 to 2005, students ages 12-18 were more likely to experience a serious violent crime away from school than at school.

- 12 – 18 years olds experienced injuries in 24% of the cases of bullying.

- 12 – 18 year olds that were bullied, 79% were bullied inside of the school building, while 28% were bullied outside on school grounds, 8% occurred more on the bus, and 5% somewhere else.

- About 28% of public and private school students ages 12-18 reported that they have been bullied at school within the past six months.

- Among high school students in grades 9-12, about 14% said they got into a fight on school property.

- 10% of male students and 6% of female students reported experiencing a threat or injury with a weapon on school property.

- Students who were being bullied, 9% of the bullying was either pushing, shoving, or tripping or spitting. The other types of bullying were verbal, exclusionary, or destruction of property.

When & Where does crime happen?

- 53% of violent crimes happen between 6 am and 6 pm.

- Almost 2/3 of rapes and sexual assaults happen at night from 6 pm to 6 am.

- Almost 1/2 happens within 1 mile from home.

- 76% happens within 5 miles of home.

- 4% of victims said that their crime took place more than 50 miles from home.

- 19% were on the streets other than those near the victims home.

- 12% happen at school.

- 8% happen at a commercial establishment.

- 22% of victims were involved in some form of leisure activity away from home at the time of being victimized.

- 22% of victims said they were at home the crime occurred.

- 20% said they were at work or traveling to or from work when the crime occurred.

- Urban residents had the highest violent victimization rates, followed by suburban resident rates. Rural residents had the lowest rates.

Because crimes of all type are going down in trend, they are still very much here and in many areas of our life. But, let's continue on some more.

Firearms & Weapons

Firearms are here to stay. So how does this affect us? Let's look how fire arms were used:

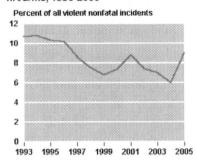

Percent of violent crimes involving firearms, 1993-2005

Percent of all violent nonfatal incidents

- In 67.9% of the nations murders

- In 42.2% of the nations robberies.

- In 21.9% of the nations aggravated assaults.

- A weapon (of some type) was used in 24% of violent crimes.

- Offenders had or used a weapon in 48% of all robberies, compared with 22% of all aggravated assaults and 7% of all rapes/sexual assaults in 2005.

- Homicides are most often committed with guns, especially handguns.

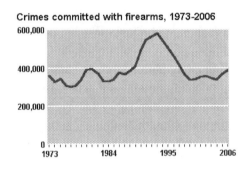

Crimes committed with firearms, 1973-2006

- 55% of homicides were committed with handguns, 16% with other guns, 14% with knives, 5% with blunt objects, and 11% with other weapons.

Chapter 2
What do you already know?

A fundamental building block of Play The Game ~ Protect Your Life is identifying and drawing upon the skills you already have. This will allow protection to be easily incorporated into your daily life.

One of my students related this analogy; from a young age you go to school and you have fire  drills. The fire drill repeated time after time prepares you to react calmly, to exit timely and orderly, how to look for the closest exit, to duck down and crawl as smoke fills the room, to touch the door and feel for heat before you open it, to STOP – DROP & ROLL if you catch on fire. By repeatedly practicing it, adding to it, and learning about it as you grow from young to old, you know what to do and how to do it. Here, we are using the same principal.

You already know ways to hurt people. Let's do an easy exercise. You will need a piece of paper and a pen or pencil.

CHALLENGE!

Now, take two minutes and write down all the ways you think you can physically hurt people.

Go!

How many did you come up with? Quite a few I would bet. Just think though, you only need one good way to make a difference. So, by only having just a few targets, you kept it simple. Simple will make it effective and easy to use. You know how to hit people, even if that is an action you would rather not think about.

As many of us have learned at some point in our early childhood, spanking is one approach  which starts us on the road to learn how to hit. However, not everyone was spanked when growing up. If you weren't, you may have known of someone who was or heard about someone who was. What is the Point? The Point is that you, through life experiences, without ever taking a martial arts class, a boxing lesson, or any other formal training, through the school of life and growing up, you learned what hitting was and how to do it.

Once again, through life's little experiences being practiced over and over again, we are conditioned to remember these experiences easily.

Have you forgotten how to play with the neighborhood kids; football, baseball, soccer, hockey, basketball, or crawling (as a baby, which I bet you can still do though you haven't done it in years) and the other so many popular sports and actions we do?

You have also already learned that when you do certain things, it hurts and that certain parts of your body can be hurt more easily than others. So, without any real training you already know where to hit if you want to inflict pain or worse. You have these skills and you are a giant step closer to mastering Play The Game ~ Protect Your Life.

CHALLENGE!

Let's challenge you again to see what you know. On the next page you will find a few simple questions. Ask yourself and your children to answer the questions. It's simple, try it. We even left space on the page for you to jot down the answers too.

What does RED generally mean when you see it?

What does YELLOW generally mean when you see it?

What does GREEN generally mean when you see it?

GREAT WORK!!! I had complete faith you could do this.

RED = STOP

If your answer is stop, danger, warning, hazard, risk, peril, threat, menace, or anything similar, you are correct.

A Red Training Band means Stop, Danger, Hit or some kind of hand Hit. You want to not let it Hit you so you will STOP it.

YELLOW = TAP

If your answer is caution, warning, care, prudence, carefulness, concern, or anything similar, you are correct.

A Yellow Training Band means caution. Because you are able to Stop the first Red hit, you could still be Hit a second time with the elbow, forearm, wrist, have the hand slip, or another part of the body unexpectedly. So, you need to be cautious after you Stop Red. Something may or may not follow.

So, Red is followed by Yellow.

GREEN = HIT

If your answer is Go, or anything similar, you are correct.

When you see Green, you want to Go. When you have a target to hit, Go for it. It's that simple. We will talk about targets again in a minute. When you Go, continue to Go without hesitation or worry, as long as, Red or Yellow aren't around to bother you. If they are, deal with them first. Then when Green comes back, Go.

Red is followed by Yellow which will eventually be followed by Green. .

So, far all of what I have talked about you should know and be able to relate to on some level. Now, I will give you something new and different.

BLUE = TRAP

Blue generally doesn't have a meaning to it. So we are using it as a safety net if you will. When you Play The Game, you will see there are many advantages to Blue because Blue is a Trap. It is a way to cut off Red and Yellow (from above).

Red is followed by Yellow, which is followed by Blue, which is followed by Green.

Red, Yellow, Blue, Green, Play The Game

Stop, Tap, Trap, Hit, Protect Your Life

The above two line express the same idea in different ways.

Don't over think this. All you need to remember are the colors which you see everyday and the meaning of these colors in everyday life. The meanings are the same in our use of them.

Target Page

CHALLENGE!

Here is a simple drawing of a person. Mark all areas that would be effective targets to inflict pain on a person in a time of self protection with a P for Point.

A Point is Green in The Game and Green means Go, which means a Hit to Protect Your Life.

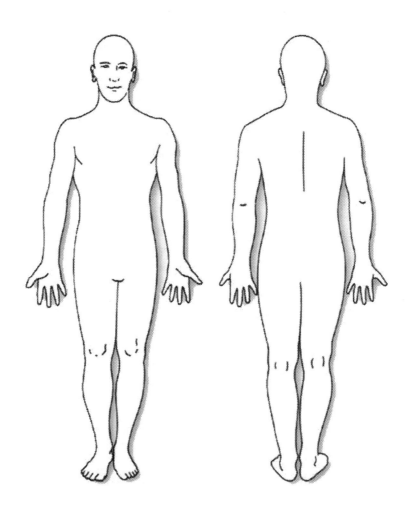

By simply reading these few pages, you have just related ideas and concepts you are already familiar with and expanded how you will use them. Using your newly refined skills you have just become *Aware*. Awareness is the first part of Play The Game ~ Protect Your Life. We practice awareness all the time, to many levels, throughout our life.

Chapter 3
Practicing Protect Your Life

Awareness – Avoidance – Action

Remember, I am using a method of teaching that allows you to relate to coordination's that you have already done. Do you know what KISS stands for? You are close; we refer to it as the "Keep It Simple System."

Play The Game ~ Protect Your Life is simple, hence KISS. Once again, you know this and the more people I talk to, the more I see the parallel in other aspects of our lives.

Let's just take this simple color analogy that is used sometimes in Awareness exercises.

White means that you are completely safe.

Gold means you have paid slight attention to things around you; you feel safe but could recognize a situation should it present itself.

Orange means your attention is on total Awareness of where you are, what is going on, who is around, and that you are giving this heightened attention to this Awareness because you believe a situation could arise.

Red means you have recognized a potential hazard or situation that is causing you to be ready for some type of action on your part. This action could be your trying to Avoid, get out of the way of, or stop the situation.

This is where Protect Your Life starts, with Red, meaning stop the threat.

Yellow means be cautious of what you are doing.

Blue means to Trap and whenever you have Trap, you go Green, which means to Hit.

The Protect Your Life aspect of our system wants you to use Yellow more often. Begin to apply Awareness – Yellow – when: you leave the house, when a stranger comes to the door, when you are driving to the store, when it is getting dark, etc… By simply being more Aware, you are more prepared. The more prepared you are, the easier it is to move up the scale and to evaluate the situation making Avoiding and Acting able to work together. By taking all of these different levels of Awareness and just being conscious of them it boils down to three simple parts:

Aware – Avoid – Act

and when confronted

Tap – Trap & Hit

CHALLENGE!

The next time you leave the house, Play this part of The Game. Take a quick look at all of the colors: White, Gold, Orange, Red, Yellow, Blue and Green. Now, as you go through whatever activities you are doing, take a second, determine what color you would be in. If you are with your children, have them tell you what color, or state of Awareness, you are at. Most times you will be at White or Gold. This is a danger zone. Because you are there so much, you let your guard down.

Be Aware!!

Awareness

Aware can be defined as having knowledge or cognizance and implies knowledge gained through one's own perceptions or by means of information. Synonyms for aware or awareness are: cognizant, conscious, sensible, awake, alert, watchful, or vigilant and would mean being mindful or heedful.

What does Awareness mean to you? What do you already know? Think about it for a moment. We want you to be aware of everything, all the time, in a casual way. You are aware when you start to get sick, when you get tired, your muscles ache and they hurt, when you are late to go somewhere, when you are hungry, thirsty, happy, sad and the list goes on and on.

Now, let's start to expand the list a little bit. How about having Awareness in trusting your instinct? Have you ever had a gut feeling? Did you ever feel something was wrong but not sure who, what, where or why? Did you ever feel a little off, uncomfortable, or leery about your surroundings or a situation? If the answer is yes, then learn to identify that feeling and learn to trust in it. Instinct is a great asset and tool, don't discard it.

Awareness leads to Avoidance. If you are Aware of a threatening situation, then it is easy to Avoid that situation which is then your Action.

CHALLENGE!

Try this exercise to start practicing Awareness through observation.

For the next week, simply focus on everyone's hands that you come in contact with. Watch how they move, where they go and how far away from them you are. Then imagine a Red dot on each hand. Could you touch that hand if you were close enough? On a piece of paper, jot a few notes down about your observations. Remember we are practicing Awareness.

Avoidance

Avoid can be defined as to stay clear of; shun, escape or to keep from happening.

Play The Game ~ Protect Your Life is meant to give you the confidence and the tools to protect yourself when confronted with a situation. The first way to prevent the occurrence is by using common sense, street smarts, or Awareness. Let's look at some examples.

You are going to the movies with your children. It is night time with a lot of activity and people milling around. You are talking and laughing, walking towards the entrance of the theater and you notice a group of teenagers some distance away. You get a feeling in your stomach, that something just isn't quite right. You see an alternative way to the entrance so you simply walk the other way. You go on to watch the movie, go for ice cream, and enjoy the evening.

By being Aware of what you felt, not sure if it was going to lead to anything in particular, you walk around the potential problem without a second thought. You have successfully Avoided & Acted together at the same time by using Awareness.

By trusting this type of Awareness and gaining confidence in trusting your instinct, many potentially dangerous situations can be Avoided by taking a simple action without hindering you from your daily family activities.

You are walking out of the mall. It is daytime in the middle of the week. You don't notice anyone around though you have a gut feeling something is going on. You are taking the keys out of your pocketbook. As you are rummaging for your keys, you notice a male approaching. He looks threatening. You take your keys and hold them in your hand with the keys between your fingers. You are not able to get into the car and he gets close enough to almost touch you. He starts asking you questions and you notice he is nervous and shaky. All of the sudden he goes to grab you and catches your coat. In an instant, you Tap, Trap & Hit the assailant in the face with your keys taking him off guard by responding so naturally and quickly, he flees.

In this example, which is what Play The Game ~ Protect Your Life is preparing you for, you were Aware of this person who was not behaving normally, you didn't have time to run away and you Avoided by preparing to Act. Then when you were left with no choice, you took Action to protect yourself.

You Avoided – kept from happening – an assault, or worse. Play The Game ~ Protect Your Life gave you the confidence not to panic and be able to take Action protecting you from danger. You responded with success and confidence, making the Action speak for itself.

I have a student who related this story and it is so typical of what we do. So I share it. Tim had graduated college and decided to go to Europe for the summer with some friends and have fun. While in Germany, Tim and his friend were shopping for jewelry and going in and out of the shops. While in one shop, they met someone who asked them if they wanted to save some money because their uncle had a shop around the corner. So, this stranger said "follow me."

Tim and his friend started following this man down an alley. Tim started to get this feeling that something wasn't right, but he and his friend kept on going. The stranger started to wind down a bunch of smaller ally's and getting ahead of him and his friend. Now, Tim is not sure how to get back to the main street they were on. To make matters worse, Tim's friend goes ahead to find the stranger and Tim is left by himself.

Finally, after a 5 minute journey he is starting to get suspicious. Tim rounds the corner, some guy comes up to him and tries to rob him. Tim gets into a fight with the guy, who is pulling on his sweatshirt. The robber gets the sweatshirt and Tim gets in a good solid punch, knocking the robber down.

Tim calls for his friend and goes down another ally and finds his friend on the ground bleeding and getting beaten by the stranger they had met on the street. Tim goes after him and the stranger runs. Tim helps his friend. But the cost was Tim's friend getting hurt and Tim losing his passport.

The moral of the story – Tim didn't trust his <u>initial instinct</u> because the stranger was so friendly. As the situation escalated, he still didn't trust his instinct. Then finally after he had no choice, the Action was finally taken because he was left with no other alternative. In this case, if he trusted in his instinct and didn't go with the stranger, this would not have happened.

He didn't trust that feeling in his gut – Awareness - that he shouldn't follow the stranger down the alley – Avoidance – and ended having to Protect - take Action. If you are Aware and then Avoid, depending on the situation, the Action will change.

Now let's apply this to Play The Game ~ Protect Your Life. Avoid as defined is "To Prevent The Occurrence" or for purpose of Play The Game ~ Protect Your Life it would be defined as simply meaning "To not get hit, Avoid the Occurrence of being struck" or Aware, Avoid, Act which is Tap, Trap, Hit.

CHALLENGE!

Try this exercise to practice Awareness and Avoiding through observation.

For the next week, simply focus on everyone's hands and arms that you come in contact with. Watch how they move, where they go and how far away from them you are. Then imagine a Red dot on each hand and a yellow dot on each arm. Could you touch that hand if you were close enough? Could you do a second or third touch if needed? On piece of paper, jot a few notes down about your observations. Remember we are practicing Awareness and Avoiding.

Action – Using Play The Game To Take Action

Quite simply put, Play The Game is a fun method of learning self protection. Protect Your Life uses what you learned in Playing The Game for a person to person attack using simple instinctive movements.

By taking the martial arts theory and removing all of the complicated movements, I replaced it with a simple, fun, easy and effective way by just Playing The Game. This game will lead to building and refining the skill of protection because it is fun to play. The more you Play The Game the better you get. The better you get, the more confident you are about the skills you obtain and it becomes second nature. Once it becomes second nature, then the appropriate Action will happen for the situation.

We hope you never have to use the Protect Your Life aspect of Playing the Game but want to see you Playing The Game often, having fun, and laughing. We want you, your children, and your parents all to be able to have the confidence that you can protect yourself because you are prepared. The way to do that is the use of a simple game that you play from time to time.

Action is what Play The Game ~ Protect Your Life is all about. If you were Aware but were unable to Avoid the situation you are left with having to deal with the situation, which is confrontation. You only have to ask yourself one question which has two possible answers:

Is this situation going to cause harm to me or my loved ones?

- If the answer is NO: Then your action is to give in. Let the robber have the money, take the car, apologize and be the bigger person to Avoid the conflict and no harm is done to anyone. Refer back to example 1 under "Avoid."

- If the answer is YES: Then your Action is to PROTECT YOURSELF. How do you protect yourself? By putting the Protect Your Life aspect of Play The Game into Action. Refer back to example 2 under Avoid.

Chapter 4
Rules for Play The Game

Play The Game is a way for everyone to practice the skill of protection so that it becomes second nature in a fun, safe, and non-aggressive way. The Game will build your confidence. The Game can be used in any situation. Once you are Aware, you can Avoid by Acting appropriately. You will be able to trust your instincts and have the confidence that you possess the protection tools needed.

Play The Game is going to show you a coordination that you have done. You can be any age, in any condition, in any position, and be able to apply it to any situation because you have already done it.

The Game is also using a method of teaching that is safe to practice and safe to use in real life.

Playing the Game

Goal

The Game is teaching you how to be protective. Be less concerned with scoring the Point and more concerned with the Tap & Trap. You will see as your Tap & Trap improves, your ability to score a Point becomes easier.

Aware and Tap & Trap is just another way for us to say Avoid which is all just protection. Become very good at it.

Scoring Points

Touch the target to score points.

A touch to each target is one point.

The first Player to get 11 hit points wins.

The better you get, the more combinations you will learn, and the longer it will take to score 11 points to win The Game.

Score more than 1 Point by Touching multiple targets at one time.

Players

Two people of any age opposing each other are needed to play The Game.

Both Players have the same objective, to protect against potential scores by the opposing Player and scoring a Point to the opposing Player.

Ages

Kids 5 – 11 comprise kindergarten to 5th grade.

Kids 12 – 18 comprise 6th grade to 12th grade.

Adults 19 – 55

Seniors 56 +

Touch

Touching is simply making light contact with another Player. You need to touch a Player in order to Play The Game. If your touch is Tapping you are Avoiding. If your Touch is on a Target, it is scoring a Point. If you can touch the Player, you can hit the opponent. So, for safety reasons we want to Touch the Player when Tapping, Trapping, or Scoring a Point.

Tap

A Tap is the touch which would Stop a Players Point while keeping in touch. But, remember this, Tap for you is an attempt to score a Point for the other Player. Taps can be done with any part of the body: hands, arms, legs, feet, body, etc…

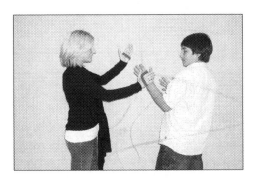

A Red Training Band means to Stop or Danger. In real life it would mean to block, deflect or redirect in some way a Hit, Punch, Palm Strike, Poke, or some type of movement that you want to Avoid.

In the first levels of The Game, we Tap primarily with the Hand or Palm. However, as you venture further into The Game you will see that any part of your body can do the Tap; for example, you can use the forearm, shoulder, hip, leg, or foot.

A Yellow Training Band means Warning, Caution, or Be Careful. Why, because some type of other step, strike, or hit may also need a Tap (Avoid or Stop) that you maybe didn't consider like a forearm, elbow, hip, knee, or foot. You want be cautious with these parts of the body as they have the potential to score a point.

A Tap implies to Stop a Player from scoring a Point. Taps are meant to teach you blocking and deflecting skills. Taps are done to Red and Yellow because they have the potential to score a Point.

Trap

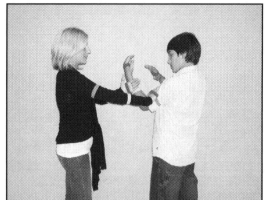

A Blue Training Band means to Trap, Hold, or cut off in some way and should be done before a scoring a Point.

A Trap can be done with the arm, leg, hip, or foot.

In real life it keeps the opponent from using that part of the body, and when crossed, from using other parts of the body. Trapping is the safest way to keep from getting hit. With practice, it will happen naturally more often than not.

A Trap also implies to gently pull or push down on some part of the body. For example, if your arm is pulled across your body because your wrist is grabbed, or Yellow, the Player is still Trapped. Another example is stepping behind the leg of a Player so moving is impossible. Then you know you have them Trapped and scored a Trip or Throw Point. Think of Trapping as your safety net.

A Trap always precedes scoring a Point. So when you get Blue, you GO Green to score a Point.

Simply think of it as:

Follow the colors, Red, Yellow, Blue, Green.

When you Touch Blue, Go Green!!!

or

Tap, Trap, Point!!!

THIS IS IMPORTANT BECAUSE IT KEEPS YOU SAFE.

Scoring Points

A Green target is a Point.

When scoring a point, LEAVE your hand on the player. When you score a point this will let the player know you scored. The person who was hit will now Tap the scoring point away and The Game continues.

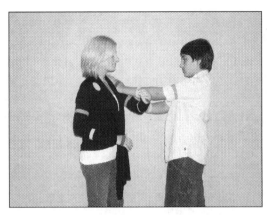

A Point implies hits, strikes, throws, locks, trips or to somehow otherwise disable the player.

A Point to the shoulder implies a strike to the head, neck, and areas above the chest, so for safety reasons, we touch the shoulder.

A Point to the body implies a strike to the mid-section or torso, or areas that are below armpit, yet above the hips. Striking vital areas such as the ribs, stomach, solar plexis, heart, kidneys, and floating ribs can damage internal organs causing injury. So again, for safety reasons, we touch the area or target.

A Point with the foot to the legs implies kicking to the groin, knees, top of the foot, or ankle.

A Point to the leg, any part, implies stepping around, moving out of the way, throwing down, upsetting the balance, or tripping.

A Point with the foot still implies hitting someone with the knee to the lower portion of the body.

Whatever you do with your arms, you can do with your legs. When Playing, you can score multiple Points at ONE time if you use your arms and legs together.

Chapter 5
Climbing Across & Away

Why, do this you say? More than anything else, what I hear most from those I have taught is, "I have no coordination" or "I will never be able to remember this." So, this simple exercise is the basis of The Game and the coordination we want you to develop. You naturally use the palm. This exercise will also make you comfortable using the back of the hand, exchanging hands, keeping in touch, and climbing or getting closer to the opposite player. As you get better at this you can practice it by seeing how fast you can do it.

It makes no difference which hand starts first as long as you do all four combinations. There is no wrong way to practice it as long as you are moving the arm across the body or away from the body.

Practice this exercise before playing The Game. Start out slow, and then go faster. See which Player can go the fastest.

CHALLENGE!

Player 2

Holds the right arm out.

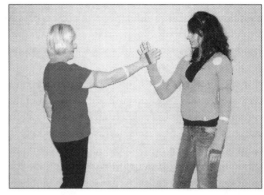

Player 2/Player 1

Player 1

As the right hand Taps Red, move the arm away while keeping in touch.

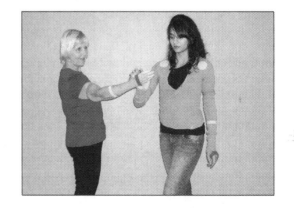

Player 1

Exchange hands to Tap Yellow while moving the arm across while keeping in touch.

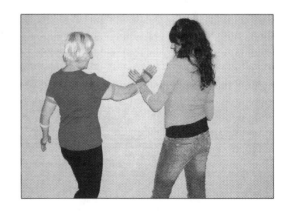

Player 1

Exchange hands to Trap Blue while
    moving the arm away while
    keeping in touch.

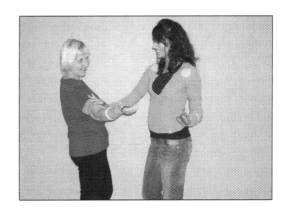

Player 1

Keep the hand on Blue and use the free
    hand to touch Green.

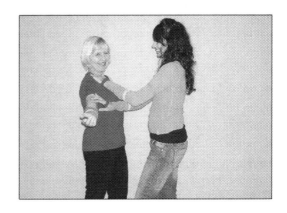

CHALLENGE!

Repeat the exercise.

Player 2

Holds the right arm out.

Player 1

As the right hand Taps Red, move the
    arm across while keeping in
    touch.

Player 1

Exchange hands to Tap Yellow, moving
    the arm away while keeping in
    touch.

Player 1

Exchange hands to Trap Blue, moving the arm across while keeping in touch.

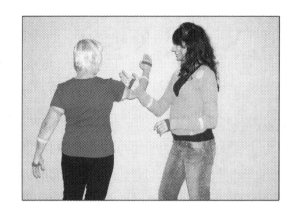

Player 1

Keep the hand on Blue and use the free hand to touch Green.

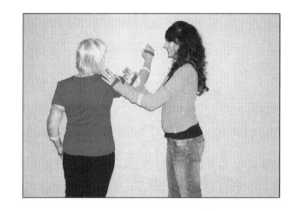

CHALLENGE!

Repeat the exercise again.

Player 2

Holds the left hand out.

Player 1

As the left hand Taps Red, move the
   arm away while keeping in
   touch.

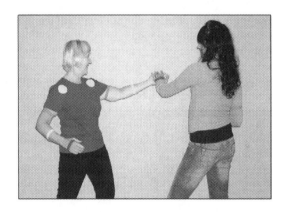

Player 1

Exchange hands to Tap Yellow, moving
   the arm across while keeping in
   touch.

Player 1

Exchange hands to Trap Blue, moving
the arm away while keeping in
touch.

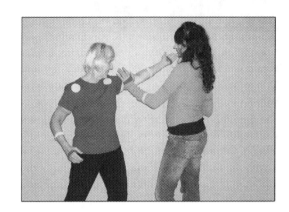

Player 1

Keep the hand on Blue and use the free
hand to touch Green.

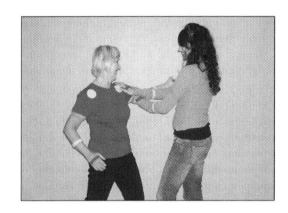

CHALLENGE!

Repeat the exercise.

Player 2

Holds the left hand out.

Player 1

As the left hand Taps Red, move the
    arm across while keeping in
    touch.

Player 1

Exchange hands to Tap Yellow, moving
    the arm away while keeping in
    touch.

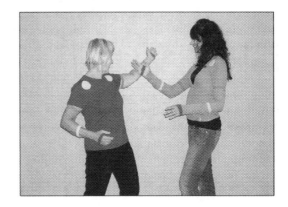

Player 1

Exchange hands to Trap Blue, moving
the arm across while keeping in
touch.

Player 1

Keep the hand on Blue and use the free
hand to touch Green.

Now, Player 1 holds out their arm and lets Player 2 Climb Across & Away.

CHALLENGE!

Now that you have practiced, see how fast each of you can do

At A Glance Climbing Across & Away 1

  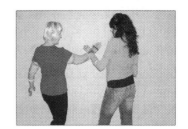

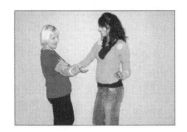 

At A Glance Climbing Across & Away 2

At A Glance Climbing Across & Away 3

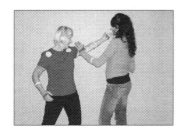 

At A Glance Climbing Across & Away 4

Chapter 6
Bone Twisting Fun!

Bone Twisting Fun

We want you to be comfortable when someone tries to grab, hold, and twist you. You need to
know how to escape and you need to know how to twist. It is as simple as In & Out,
Long & Short.

Escape

You Escape when a Player grabs you. Tap to remove the color that is applying the twist. It
will usually be Red or Yellow you need to remove.

Thumbs Out Long

When grabbing the thumb side of the hand, simply turn away from the Player. Long allows
      you to control and move a Player.

Player 2

Put your right hand on Player 1 at the
      Point target.

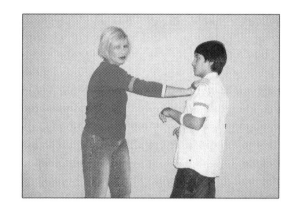

Player 1

Take your left hand and grab the
      thumb side of the hand.

Player 1

Twist the thumb away. You did it, Point!

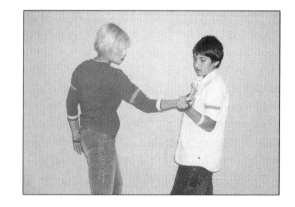

At A Glance – Thumbs Out Long

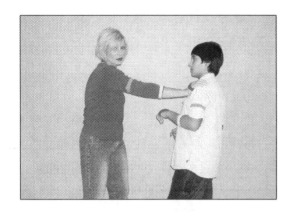 

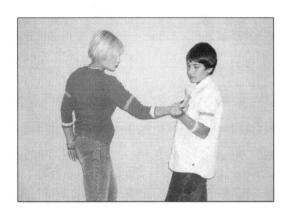

CHALLENGE!

There might be the occasion when you twist with one hand; it isn't enough to move the Player. When that happens, use your free hand and add to it or "Plus."

Player 2

Put your right hand on Player 1 at the
      Point target.

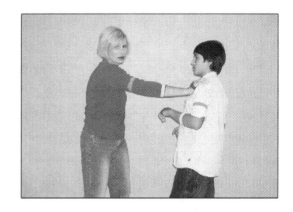

Player 1

Take your right hand and grab the thumb
      side of the hand.

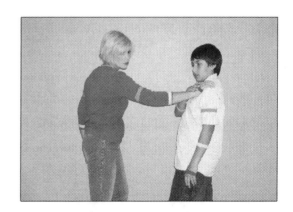

Player 1

Twist the thumb away, but it isn't making
      the Player move.

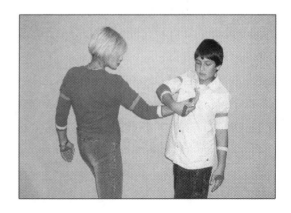

Player 1

Use the free hand to add to it or Plus, now
    you have the Point!

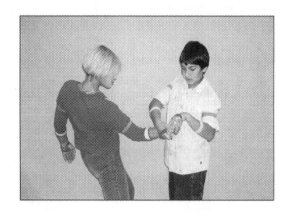

At A Glance – Thumbs Out Long Plus

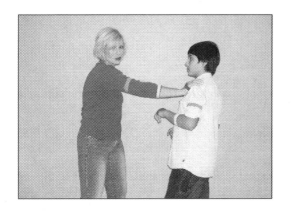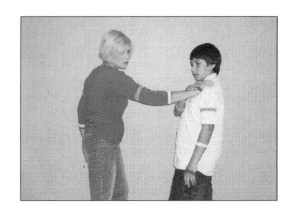

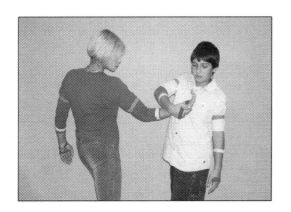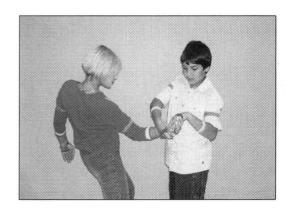

CHALLENGE!

Thumbs Out Short

By making a Players arm short, or close to their body allows you to create discomfort; and if done with enough force, pain. So, go slow and easy with this challenge to avoid hurting your partner.

Player 2

Put your right hand on Player 1 at the Point target.

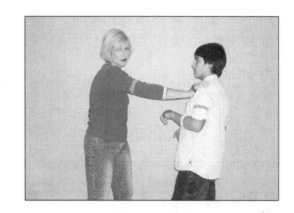

Player 1

Take your left hand and grab the thumb side of the hand.

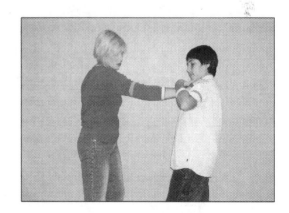

Player 1

Twist the Player's hand bring it close to their body. You did it, Point!

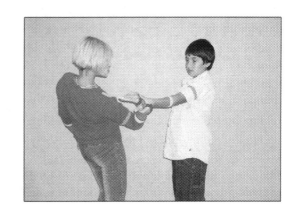

At A Glance – Thumbs Out Short

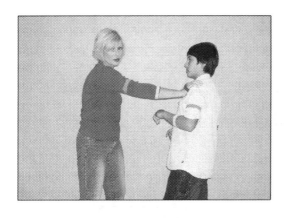

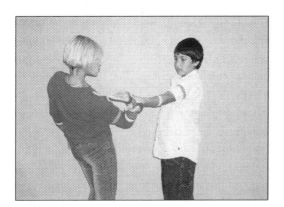

CHALLENGE!

Thumb Out Short Plus

Player 2

Put your right hand on Player 1 at the
     Point target.

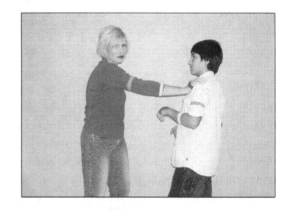

Player 1

Take your left hand and grab the thumb
     side of the hand.

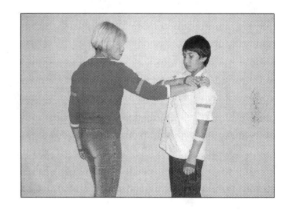

Player 1

Twist the Player's hand and use the free
     hand to add to it or Plus, now you
     have the Point!

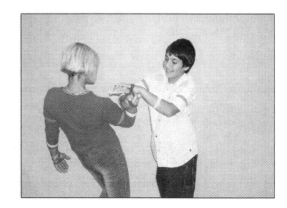

At A Glance – Thumbs Out Short Plus

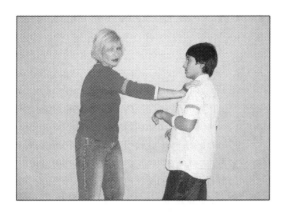
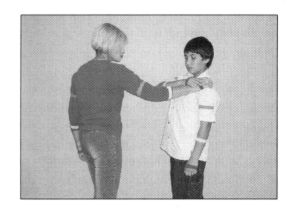

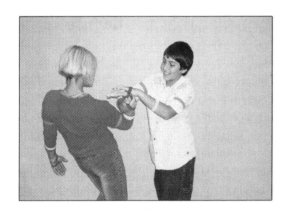

CHALLENGE!

Pinkies In Long

When grabbing the pinky side of the hand, simply turn the pinky into the Player. Long allows you to control and move a Player

Grab the pinky side and Twist In.

Player 1

Put your left hand on Player 2 at the Point target.

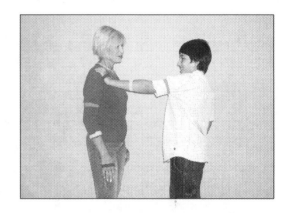

Player 2

Take your left hand and grab the Pinky side of the hand.

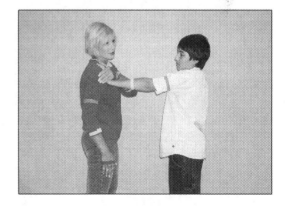

Player 2

Twist the Pinky in. You did it, Point!

At A Glance – Pinkies In Long 1

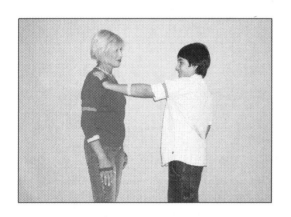

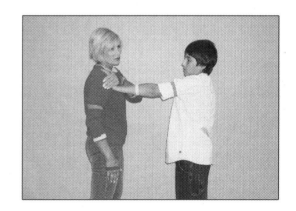

CHALLENGE!

Player 1

Put your left hand on Player 2 at the Point target.

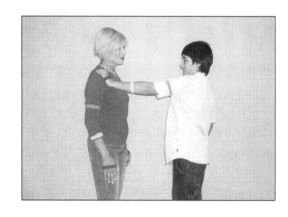

Player 2

Take your right hand and grab the Pinky side of the hand.

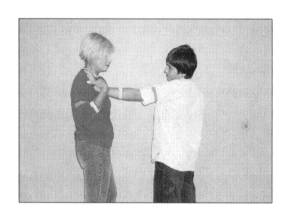

Player 2

Twist the Pinky in, turn your body if you need too. You did it, Point!

At A Glance – Pinkies In Long 2

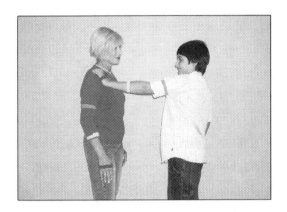

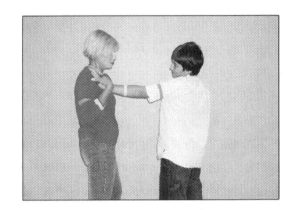

CHALLENGE!

Pinkies In Short

Short allows you to create discomfort.

Player 1

Put your left hand on Player 2 at the Point
      target.

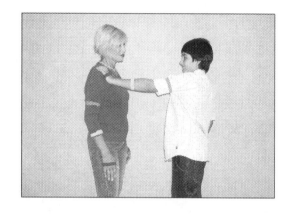

Player 2

Take your left hand and grab the Pinky
      side of the hand.

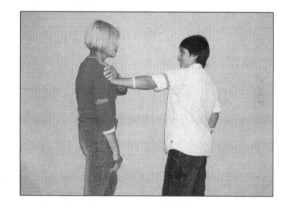

Player 2

Twist the Pinky in bringing it close to
      Player 1. You did it, Point!

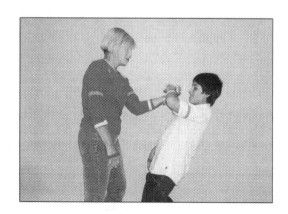

At A Glance – Pinkies In Short 1

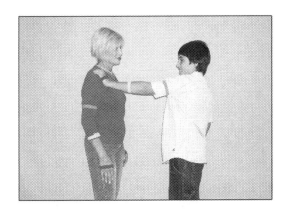

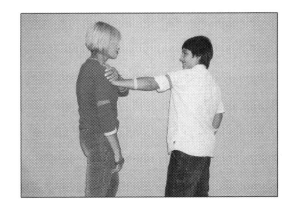

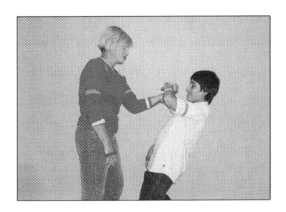

CHALLENGE!

Pinkies In Short

Player 1

Put your left hand on Player 2 at the Point target.

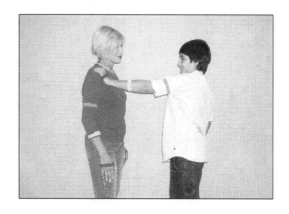

Player 2

Take your right hand and grab the Pinky side of the hand.

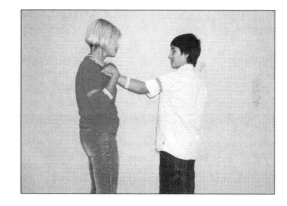

Player 2

Twist the Pinky in bringing it close to Player 1. You did it, Point!

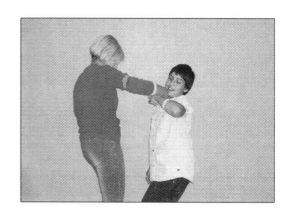

CHALLENGE!

Now, repeat this challenge with each Player using the other hand.

At A Glance – Pinkies In Short 2

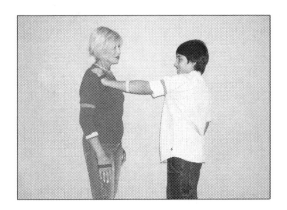
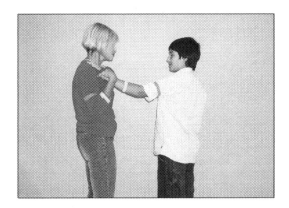

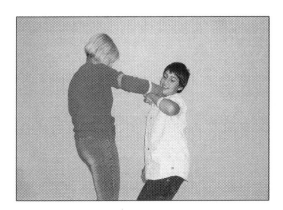

Chapter 7
Play The Game

Starting Challenge

Each Player will do the following
steps:

1. Smile

2. Relax

3. Go Slow

4. Have Fun - it's a Game

Player 1/Player 2

Each Player holds their arms out, thumbs up, places a Red training band around each hand.

Each Player places a Green sticker on each shoulder.

Stand, sit or position across from each other at arms distance apart

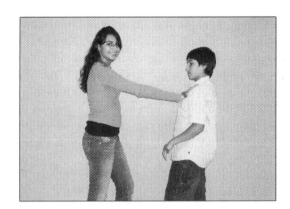

Each Player will take their hand and touch Red training band to Red training band. Which hand each Player uses doesn't matter.

Play The Game

Easiest Challenge

From the Starting Level, Player 1 using their free hand, going slowly tries to score a point on Player 2. Player 2 uses a Tap to Red to stop Player 1 from scoring the point.

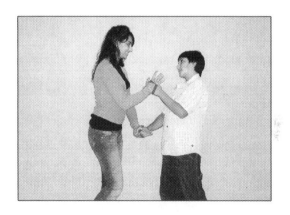

Each Player, at the same time, continues exchanging hands using one hand to Tap the Red, to stop the point, and the free hand trying to score a point.

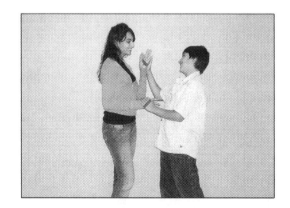

Each Player continues to Tap trying to score a point.

There is no right or wrong number of times that it takes to score the point. The better you get, the longer it will take.

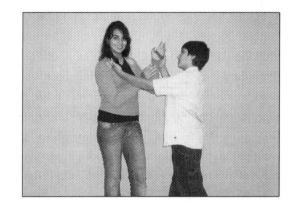

Player 2 goes to score a point.

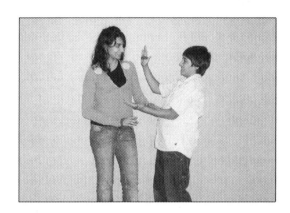

Player 1 Taps Red and stops the point. If you stopped the point, you were successful.

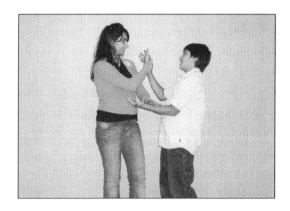

Player 1 scores a point, Excellent!
Keep playing this level.
The first Player to score 11
points wins!!

At A Glance Easiest Level

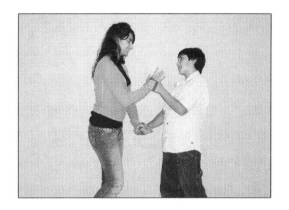
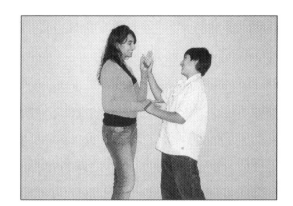
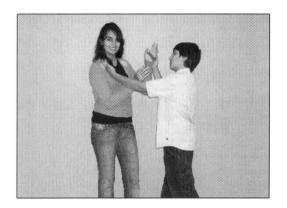
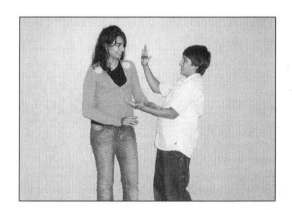
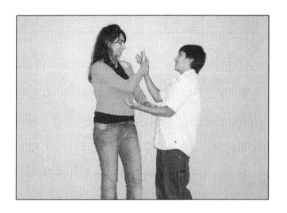

Easier Challenge

Each Player will put their arms out with thumbs up and place a Yellow training band on the middle of each forearm.

Start.

This time we are adding the Yellow training band to the game.

Player 2 uses a Tap to Yellow to stop Player 1.

The objective now is for each player to Tap the next **closest** Red or Yellow training band on either arm.

Player 1 goes to Tap Yellow on Player 2.

Player 2 responds by going to the next **closest** Red or Yellow training band on Player 1.

Player 2 uses the free hand to try to score a point. Player 1 Taps the Red to stop the point.

Remember, Taps are stops to Red & Yellow.

Player 1 uses the bottom hand to Tap Yellow.

If you see the opportunity to score a point, try it.

Maintain an even speed as you play.

Continue to exchange Taps with each other.

Remember there is no wrong number of Taps and no wrong way to Tap.

Player 1 scores a point; Excellent! Keeping your hand on the Green, let Player 2 Tap it off. Continue to Play The Game.

The first Player to score 11 points wins!!

At A Glance Easier Level

Easy Challenge

Each Player will put their arms out with thumbs up and place a Blue training band around the middle of each upper arm.

Stand, sit or position across from each other at arms distance apart

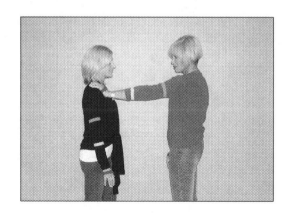

Start. This time we are adding a Blue
training band to the game.

Player 1 uses a Tap to stop Player 2 at
Yellow.

**Don't try to score a point
unless you have a Trap to the
Blue training band. At this
Level, no points are scored
unless you have Blue to Trap.**

Player 2 does a Tap to Player 1 on
        Yellow and tries for a Trap to
        Blue.
        Remember:
        Go Slow & Even
        Work your way up the arm
        Try to Trap on Blue

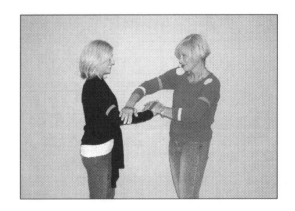

Player 2 Traps on Blue. Player 1 uses their free hand to Trap Player 2.
You can skip Yellow and go directly to Blue.

Remember, your goal is to Trap Blue without getting hit by the Red or the Yellow.

Player 2 Taps Player 1 on Yellow while still Trapping Blue.

Player 2 continues holding Yellow, while using the other hand to Trap Blue. Player 1 also Traps Blue on Player 2.
GO SLOWLY
Play The Game, let it flow.
You should be doing 1 or 2 Taps followed by a Trap.
When you Trap on Blue try to score a point.

Player 1 scores a point, Excellent!
Keeping your hand on the Green,
let Player 2 Tap it off. Continue to
Play The Game.

The first Player to score 11 points
wins!!

This is the most important level of Playing The Game. At this level, you are using fundamental skills and preparing for challenging variations.

This is as simple as playing Tic Tac Toe!!

At A Glance Easy Level

 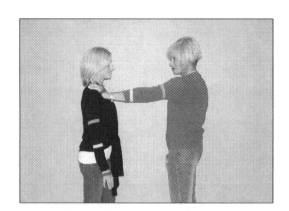

 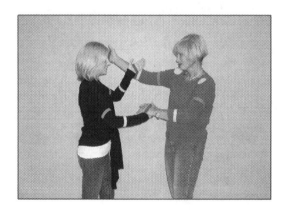

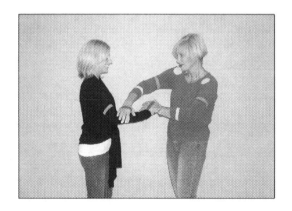 

Chapter 8
Protecting Your Life

Real Life Scenario's

Below you will find exactly how this is meant to work. Through the use of real life, everyday situations that confront us, we will show you how to Play The Game to Protect Your Life. When the time comes, all you will have to remember is "The Game," "Red, Yellow, Blue, Green," or "Tap – Trap & Hit." Through this simple yet effective method, you will be able to protect yourself against almost any situation.

Aware, Avoid, Act, Always Look & Play
Red, Yellow, Blue, Green, Learn To Play The Game
One, Two, Three, Four, Play The Game With Family & More

Aware, Avoid, Act, It Is Still The Same
Stop, Tap, Trap, Hit, To Protect Your Life
As Simple, Easy, & Fun as Tic, Tac, Toe

You did it because of What YOU Already know!

The Bully Push & Shove

Push & Shove

You are playing on the playground at
school during recess.

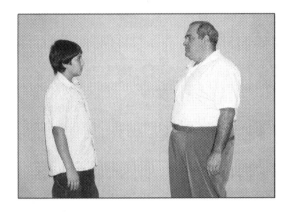

Another child on the play ground comes
over and starts bullying you.

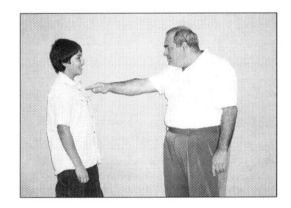

They start pushing and shoving you
around.

You tell them to stop, they don't.

You get pushed.

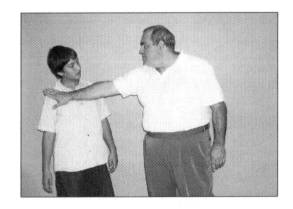

You act by Tapping! the forearm away.

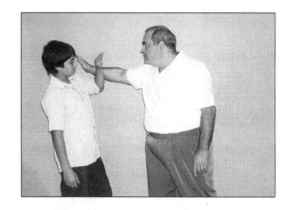

The push again, at the same time. You respond with another Tap!

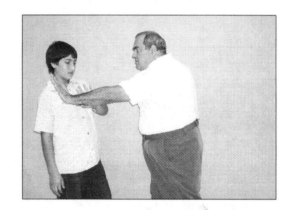

They try one more time, you Tap! again and with one good push away, send the bully off balance tripping backwards. You "Protected Your Life!"

Stop! Tap! Trap! Hit!

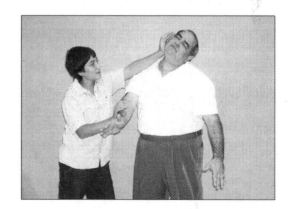

At A Glance The Bully Push & Shove

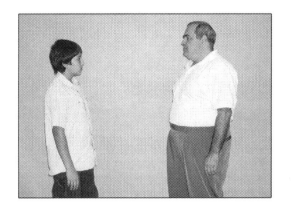 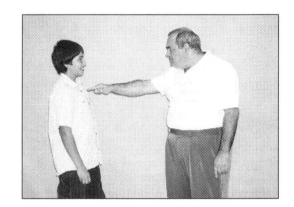

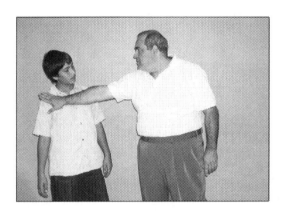 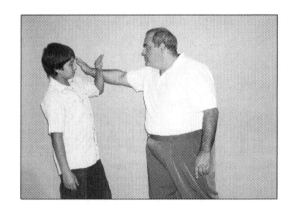

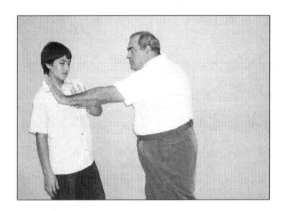 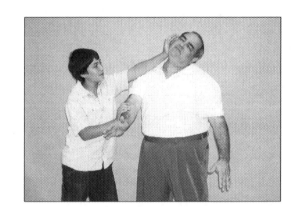

The Fist Fight

Fist Fight

A punch is thrown at you. You Stop! the
hand that is punching.

A second punch is thrown at you. You
Tap!

The free hand is used to Trap! pushing the upper arm against the body and Trapping it.

You Hit! with the free hand to the face. You "Protected Your Life!"

At A Glance The Fist Fight

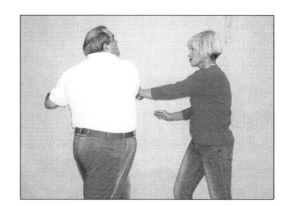

Man Follows Woman

You go out with your husband for a relaxing dinner at a local restaurant. You have a seat at a table. You're having a good time, enjoying a great meal and conversation. It has been a long time since you have been out. You are calm and in a safe place that you have enjoyed dinner before with your family. You need to use the Ladies Room. You excuse yourself and go to the other side of the restaurant. You walk into the Ladies Room and out of nowhere a man walks into the Ladies Room behind you and grabs you around the neck.

Man follows woman into the Ladies Room

You get grabbed from behind around the neck.

You react in a natural manner, one hand Stops!/Grabs the hand

Your other hand Taps! the elbow.

You use your whole body pulling your head out, pulling the hand around your neck, and continuing to Trap! the elbow.

You are now behind the person, with your hand still Trapping! the elbow, and you hand is pushing the other persons hand up to his neck. It creates an intense pain and you have "Protected Your Life."

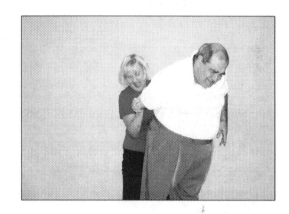

At A Glance Man Follow A Woman

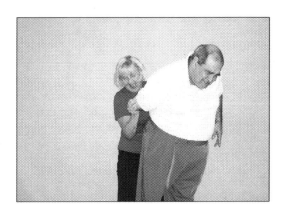

Interesting Websites

http://www.mcgruff.org

http://www.ojp.usdoj.gov/ovc/help/welcome.html

http://www.colorquiz.com/title.html

Bibliography/References

- Dr. Gary S. Torres, MD – Pa Kua Chuan Theory & Application DVD's, Tai Chi Push Hands Applications & Theory DVD's, 9 Alley Theory & Application's DVD & Workshop.

- Indicators of School Crime & Safety 2006 – Institute of Education Sciences, National Center for Education Statistics.

- US Department of Justice, Office of Justice Programs, Bureau of Justice Statistics website http://www.ojp.usdoj.gov/bjs/

- US Department of Justice, Federal Bureau of Investigation, Criminal Justice Information Services Division, 2006 Crime in the United States, website http://www.fbi.gov/ucr/cius2006/offenses/violent_crime/index.html

- Federal Bureau of Investigation http://www.fbi.gov/ucr/cius2006/index.html

- Department of Justice - http://www.ojp.usdoj.gov/bjs/cvict_c.htm

- Talking With The Kids http://www.talkingwithkids.org/nickelodeon/pr-3-8-01.htm

- http://www.aware.org/crimes.shtml

- http://www.fbi.gov

- http://www.crime-reg.com/ressources/misconceptions.htm

- http://www.nocensorship.us/color_of_crime.html

- In The Gravest Extreme – The Role of the Firearm in Personal Protection, by Massad F. Ayoob

- http://www.safereturntraining.com

- http://educationalissues.suite101.com/article.cfm/color_and_learning

- http://www.llrx.com/columns/guide56.htm

- http://www.colorquiz.com/about.html

- http://www.learningincolor.com/faq.htm

- http://www.pesoftware.com/Resources/moveLearn.html#learn

- http://www.lextreme.com/rt.html